Dolls' House Bathrooms

Lots of Little Loos

Dolls' House Bathrooms
Lots of Little Loos

Patricia King

Guild of Master Craftsman Publications Ltd

First published 1997 by
Guild of Master Craftsman Publications Ltd,
166 High Street, Lewes,
East Sussex, BN7 1XU

ISBN 1 86108 056 5

Photographs by Steve Hawkins

Cover photographs by Steve Hawkins

Line drawings by Roderick King

Designed by Ed White Design & Print

Typeface: Bembo

Origination in Singapore under the supervision of
MRM Graphics, Winslow, Buckinghamshire, UK
Printed in Hong Kong by H & Y Printing Ltd.

I would like to dedicate this book to
Ian, Amanda, Roderick and Colin.

Acknowledgements

I have found myself in a new world - the secret life of loos -
and I would like to thank the following people for their help and
enthusiasm in steering me through it:

J. Hadleigh Marlow Pritchard, author of *Sanatoria Hygenas*;
Len Blackmore, who collects these wonderful creations; and
Tony Swane and Tim Cooper from Drummonds of Bramley,
who sell them!

To Alan Phillips for believing in my ability. And to Liz Inman
and Lindy Dunlop for their encouragement and informed help.

Contents

Foreword

It has been a delight to work with Patricia King over the years, editing her magazine columns, for she has never ceased to amuse me. So I know you are in for a treat when you pick up her latest book. Not only will it inspire you to tackle her imaginative projects, you'll start looking at the world through different eyes. You will also find it highly entertaining: her infectious enthusiasm for life is equalled only by her wit and sense of humour, which more than comes over in her writing. And I'm sure the subject of little loos offers her plenty of scope and irresistible opportunities for her zany games of word play. Her flair for making miniature masterpieces out of junk and bric-a-brac is astounding. Her fertile and inventive imagination is set loose with the challenge of making scenes using throwaway household objects. After reading her pieces you will start seeing ordinary objects, such as baby's bottle teats or coffee stirrers, in a new light. It's fun to actually study the photographs of her models and see if you can spot the items she made each out of before reading how she did it.

She is a flamboyant personality, she adores vibrant colour all around her - in her home, craft work, and also in her clothes. You will rarely miss her in a crowd. One word of warning though, if you do happen to meet up - just don't try to keep up with her. I spent an unforgettable weekend with her at Miniatura and was absolutely exhausted at the end of it. My ribs ached from laughing.

Jackie Unwin
Editor, *Dolls' House World*

Introduction

Before you even start on any model in this book, perhaps you should examine what sort of person you are because, it seems to me, if you are the quiet, structured type, you may not make any of them! I am not doubting your modelling ability - that's the easy part - it is the awkward situations you can get into while acquiring materials that I am worried about. If you're not ready with an explanation as to why you want things, you may come a cropper! I am an extrovert, and going about the quest for unusual makings with interesting potential is half the fun for me: I roam the chemists, supermarkets and ironmongers with an eye more for the packaging than the product.

Take Tinklebell's toilet for instance. There is very little in the way of research about where fairies go - in fact, there is a rumour that they don't go at all - so I reasoned that their loos must not only be small, but also very well disguised. (Agreed? Well, it's only logical isn't it?) Therefore, I looked for a natural object to house it in.

I started by hollowing out a coconut, then I tried to dry a squash (now I know why they are so named). Finally, I decided what I needed was a dried gourd. I asked at garden centres and flower shops, even at art schools, and I had such a hard time finding one that I am half inclined to write an odyssey of my efforts entitled *Nearer my Gourd to Thee*.

The first question everybody asked was 'what is a Gourd?', the second, 'what do you want it for?' (Pause here, dear reader, in case you should find yourself in a similar situation, and consider whether the questioner is resilient enough to take the answer in their stride.) Me? I told them, 'I am making a dolls' house fairies' loo and I need a gourd to house it in.' I would begin trustingly…The reactions were

1

predictable, but I am pleased to report that the men from the funny farm still haven't come for me with one of their long-sleeved white coats.

It may be my fault that you are lying, even now, half buried in bars of soap on the supermarket floor. I was the one who removed the shaped tray that they formerly sat in, and then piled them up in a teetering pyramid on the shelf of the supermarket. I bore the tray off to the checkout and asked if I could have it. Fortunately, this time all I got was a perfunctory nod, so I was spared from explaining that it would be a perfect miniature urinal!

Later, at college, I realized that the pre-formed tray that oil paint tubes are packed in would suit my purpose even better, so I asked the secretary if she could spare one or two. She wanted to know what I wanted to use them for, and when I explained about the miniature urinal, this lass not only took the whole thing in her stride and gave me the trays, she went on to ask if I had seen the Victorian loo locked away in a remote part of the building, and producing a bunch of keys that would have done credit to a prison warder, she led me to a locked room where they stored one of the handsomest toilet creations I have ever seen. (College staff are special in that way: nothing phases them!)

Being privy (if you will excuse the expression) to this sort of privilege is just one of the benefits of this sort of modelling. You never know where you will find the bits and pieces and the models, when completed, are a bit like a patchwork quilt - they not only look right, they also remind you of where you found their components and the people who are on your wavelength and helped you in their creation.

CHAPTER

1

TECHNIQUES
AND MATERIALS

Tools and Safety

I feel a bit diffident at offering advice in this realm. In my opinion, all tools are set implacably against all humans. It's war and I know it! My incompetence with specialist tools is probably responsible for my developing the style of modelling I have. I only use a handful of tools. Modelling for me is essentially a table-top hobby and I want to keep it simple. The tools I find indispensable are:

- craft knives
- steel rule
- cutting mat
- pliers
- tweezers

- scissors
- small saw
- leather punch
- vice (I also use clothes pegs to hold things together)
- small electric drill (wear protective goggles when you use this)
- nail files and emery boards
- glue gun

GLUE GUNS

Glue guns are thermostatic and work by heating a stick of solid glue and letting the resulting viscous glue out at a controlled rate. You must treat them with respect as the glue is very hot and can cause a nasty blister if dropped on the skin, but it doesn't set for a couple of seconds, which gives you a bit of fiddle time, and the resultant bond is good. You can also make a tiny pad from the glue so that you can stick a

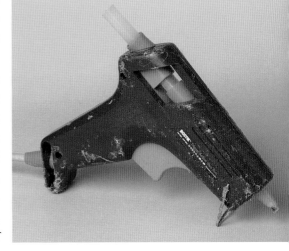

round object onto a flat surface. Don't get a very small glue gun – they look dinky, but they are underpowered.

You will need other glues for spreading over large areas, as for wallpapering, and the best adhesive I have found for this sort of work is Copydex. It is good with both paper and fabric. Adding a drop of water to Copydex will make it go further. Copydex also has the advantage of enabling you to unstick things that you have stuck together. However, be careful not to get it on your clothes as it is a rubber solution and hardens immediately. There is a Copydex remover, but even if you buy it, it's never there when you need it! If you do get Copydex on your clothes, dilute it with lots of water before it sets completely.

PAINTS

For a good, all over cover, I find car spray paints are invaluable. They give instant colour, get in all the nooks and crannies, and the paint dries quickly and has a nice shine. However, if you are using a light colour - particularly white - you need to use a primer first. Try the metallic sprays for dark browns.

There are two types of car spray paint: I like the cellulose sprays, but acrylics are also available and they work out much cheaper than those sold exclusively for modelling. Do not spray cellulose and acrylic on the same piece or the paint will peel and flake off.

Spray paints are dangerous if inhaled, so they should never be used in a confined space. I spray my models in the garden, and always wear a paper face mask. These are available for a few pence wherever car spray paints are sold.

Tubes of acrylic paints are very good and have the advantage of being waterproof when they dry.

Shiny surfaces can be painted with

watercolours if you drag the paintbrush over a bar of domestic soap before you dip it in the colour. To make it permanent, go over the colour with a coat of varnish.

VARNISH

I use household polyurethane varnish which comes in small tins of gloss, matt or satin. Always clean the brush immediately after using varnish or rigor mortis will set in. Use thinners if you have them, but nail polish remover will work just as well. Follow up with a wash in soapy water. Turps or white spirit will not remove enamel or cellulose.

I often use a quick decoupage technique – if you want a tiny floral pattern to decorate a loo bowl or cistern, it works quite well. Cut out paper motifs, stick them to the piece to be decorated, and varnish over them again and again until they appear to be part of the original. In true decoupage you rub down each coat before applying the next – me? I can't wait that long. I find two or three coats with no rubbing down adequate.

Finding Materials

Using found objects to make models means you can achieve elaborate details without much effort, and of course, with multiple items (like the four legs of a chair), uniformity is assured. But, unless you have a button box the size of a room, you will have to acquire this wherewithal: jumble sales, boot fairs and charity shops make wonderful searching grounds in the hunt for likely bits and pieces. It is often the unexpected thing you see and buy that sparks your imagination to making something you had never thought of before.

It is surprising how often the bubble packs in chemists and DIY stores provide useful shapes that set you thinking, and many is the time the King family has had to use a product because of the pack it came in! Any customs officer opening my suitcase on my return from a holiday abroad would come to the conclusion that I am a secret drinker, as I frequently return with the free miniature bottles – empty – given to me and to everyone else on the plane within persuading reach!

You need to be a bit of a hoarder to enjoy this sort of modelling because you never know when that bottletop you picked up will come in handy. I have listed some of the materials that I find useful below, and given examples of how I use them, but don't limit yourself to these suggestions - almost anything can be used!

BRACKETS AND SUPPORTS

Cake tier pillars: *loo and washbasin stands*
Chesspieces: *washbasin stands*
Filigree link belts: *washstand supports*
Filigree fan: *brackets and washstand supports*
Turned cocktail sticks: *washstand and seat supports*

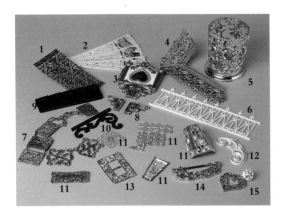

1   Filigree panel
2   Filigree plastic fan
3   Sconce from Barbie doll roundabout
4   Section of elaborate picture frame
5   Plastic cup holder
6   Dolls' house railing
7   Lozenges from chain belt
8   Quarters cut from square pendant
9   Pressed-out label holders
10 Section of plastic picture frame
11 Filigree panels from jewellery findings
12 Stick-on furniture decoration
13 Buckle
14 Half a buckle
15 Earring with drop

GENERAL FIXTURES AND FITTINGS

Record racks: *municipal toilet roofs*

Balsa wood strip: *almost anything*

Shampoo nozzles and eye dropper bottles: *to link downpipes and cisterns*

Solder: *downpipes and taps*

Plastic spout from fruit juice carton: *toilet seat*

Fine chains and beads: *chains and handles*

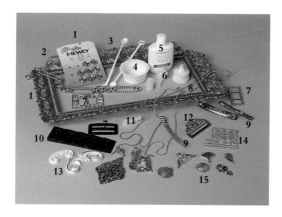

1 Press studs
2 Long link chain belt
3 McDonald's coffee stirrers
4 Individual portion jam tub
5 Hand cream container
6 Hair dye nozzle
7 Fancy buckle
8 Fine chains

9   Parts from child's hair slide
10 Pressed-out label holders
11 Rawlplug
12 Part of nurse's buckle
13 Stick-on furniture decoration
14 Filigree moulding
15 Parts of drop earrings

CISTERNS

Use any of the objects listed below as cisterns.
If you want a 'wooden' cistern, it is best to make it up from
stripwood and/or card.

Individual portion butter tubs
Square bean slicer
Amplex or sweetener pocket dispensers
Birdcage seed hoppers
Small boxes with lids
Plastic aspirin and codeine bottles
Cycle puncture outfit box
Plastic miniature drinks bottles
Room freshener container (Haze boxes
    are a good shape)
Plastic toothbrush box

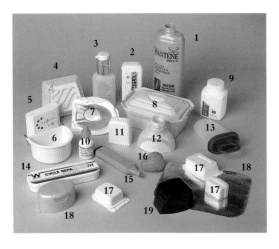

1   Shampoo bottle
2   Amplex dispenser
3   Pocket face cream dispenser
4   Haze room freshener
    container
5   Hotel soap container
6   Birdcage seed hopper
7   Packaging from refrigerator
    deodorant egg
8   Pâté box
9   Plastic aspirin bottle
10 Eye drop bottle
11 Pocket sweetener dispenser
    (lower part)
12 Shampoo bottle (top part)
13 Iced lolly mould
14 Bicycle puncture kit
15 Stabilo Boss highlighter
16 Walnut shell
17 Single portion butter tubs
18 Shampoo bottle top
19 Scent bottle lid

LOO BOWLS

Any of the items below can be 'transformed' into admirable loo bowls, the last two into men's urinals.

Hanging shower gel tops
Plastic salt cellar
Ice lolly moulds
Shampoo tops
Individual portion cream and milk tubs
Eye baths, egg cups and plastic eggs
Packaging from refrigerator deodorant eggs
Small plastic bottles, e.g. for aspirins
Deodorant tubes
Walnuts
Hair dye nozzle
Plastic cylinders
Twin-packs for éclairs
Six-packs of tube paints

1 Six-pack for acrylic or
   oil paints
2 Twin-pack for éclairs
3 Plastic egg
4 Small metal egg cup
5 Deodorant tube
6 Cake pillar
7 Hanging shower
   gel top
8 Pâté container
9 Packaging from
   refrigerator deodorant
   egg
10 Half a cake pillar
11 Individual portion milk
   or cream tub
12 Half a plastic egg
13 Eye bath
14 Iced lolly mould

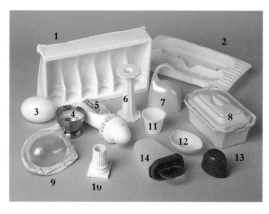

CHAPTER

2

HIGH FLUSH
LOOS

The Magnificent Dolphin

This W.C. is so magnificent that I'm not sure anyone who doesn't boast the surname 'King' (as I do!) has any right to model it. In case you insist, we print a picture of the original to show you how awesome it is.

MATERIALS

Fimo
Handbag clasp
Card
Balsa
Brass nut
Jewellery findings (2)
Long link from a chain belt
Kinder egg ($\frac{1}{2}$)
Keyhole cover
Copper or brass wire
Necklace fasteners (2)
Fine chain
Brass foil
Decorative brooch setting

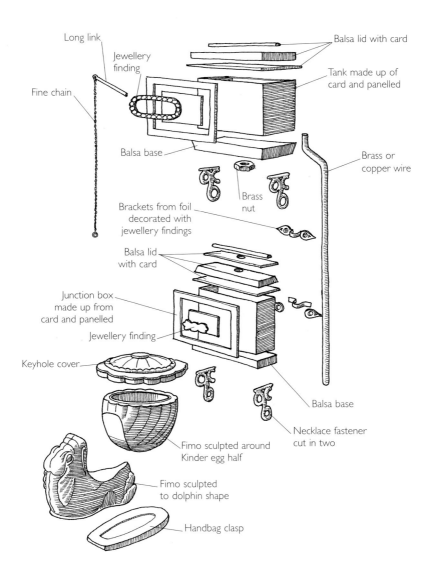

Long link

Jewellery finding

Fine chain

Balsa lid with card

Tank made up of card and panelled

Balsa base

Brass or copper wire

Brass nut

Brackets from foil decorated with jewellery findings

Balsa lid with card

Junction box made up from card and panelled

Jewellery finding

Keyhole cover

Balsa base

Necklace fastener cut in two

Fimo sculpted around Kinder egg half

Fimo sculpted to dolphin shape

Handbag clasp

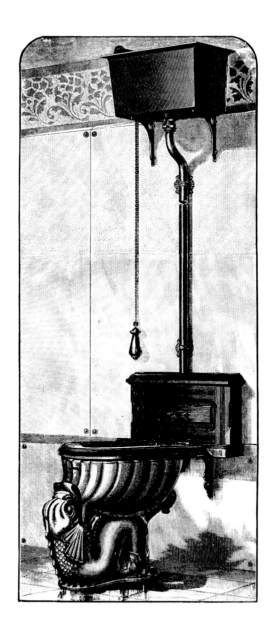

The 'Dolphin.' Ivory-
tinted porcelain. Design
patented.

METHOD

1 Cover the half Kinder egg with Fimo and model grooves around it. Shape up a sausage of Fimo and bend it into shape to make the waste pipe. Model it to look like an open-mouthed dolphin. Bake the Fimo to harden it, following the instructions on the Fimo packet. The plastic Kinder egg will melt, but as it doesn't show, leave it!

2 Mount the whole assembly on the handbag clasp. Paint and varnish the dolphin.

3 Paint the keyhole cover brown and top the open loo with it.

4 Make up two boxes from card, one for the cistern and the other for the junction box. Panel both boxes and add jewellery findings as the central ornaments. Top both boxes with balsa lids, layered with card, and finish each with a balsa base.

5 Add necklace fasteners cut in two as brackets to support both boxes.

6 Attach a length of fine chain to a long link. Pierce the side of the cistern and glue the link in place.

7 Drill a hole in the top of the junction box and insert the copper wire. Attach the nut underneath the cistern. Bend the pipe to a realistic shape, adjust its height and insert it into the nut.

8 Stain the boxes brown and set the completed W.C. in place on the wall.

9 Cut short lengths of brass foil, bend them to shape, and use them to band the pipe to the wall. Make them even more elaborate by adding the little fleur-de-lis that often hold stones in brooches.

17

The Goliath

For really elaborate moulding on the pedestal, dig out your old jewellery findings and earring drops, and glue them all over the pedestal.

MATERIALS

Hanging shower gel lid
Earring drops
Curves from a decorative
    plastic photo frame
Bendy plastic straw
Canary's seed hopper
Child's hair slide closer
Giftwrap
Thin card
Balsa
Bugle beads (2)
Fine chain
Bead
Nozzle from hair dye
    container
Individual butter portion tub
Belthole eyelet
Paper towel holder
Jewellery finding

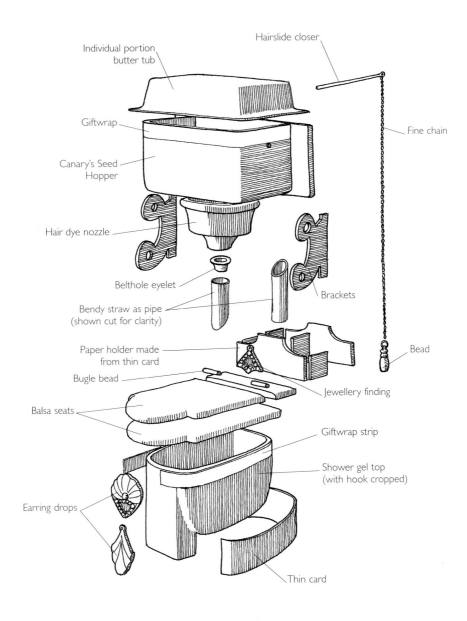

Individual portion
butter tub

Hairslide closer

Giftwrap

Fine chain

Canary's Seed
Hopper

Hair dye nozzle

Belthole eyelet

Brackets

Bendy straw as pipe
(shown cut for clarity)

Paper holder made
from thin card

Bead

Bugle bead

Jewellery finding

Balsa seats

Giftwrap strip

Shower gel top
(with hook cropped)

Earring drops

Thin card

METHOD

1 Turn gel lid upside down and cut off end of curve.

2 Cut thin card to make a pedestal, using the gel curve as the flat front piece. Glue the pedestal pieces together and decorate the pedestal with earring drops.

3 Spray the pedestal white to blend the stuck-on decorations with the background. Band across the top and bottom with a strip of motifs cut from giftwrap.

4 Pick out the pattern of the earring drops with blue acrylic paint and varnish the whole pedestal.

5 Make two seats from balsa. Cut the top seat at the back and insert bugle beads into the cut for hinges. Glue both seats onto the pedestal.

6 Cut out the paper towel holder and glue it in place at the back of the seat. Decorate the holder with a jewellery finding.

7 Trim a bendy straw to length for a downpipe and attach it to the back of the pedestal. Top the downpipe with a belthole eyelet.

8 Cut a strip of giftwrap and wind it around the seed hopper. Drill a hole in the side of the hopper to take the chain. Attach a length of chain to the child's hair slide closer, and cut the chain to the required length. Attach a bead to the other end of the chain, glue the open end of the hair slide closer into the hole in the hopper, and top the hopper with the butter tub, upside down. Add brackets to support the hopper (shown on right side only in photo).

9 Glue the hair dye nozzle underneath the hopper, and fix the downpipe to this, shaping and trimming it as required.

For details of loo roll holder, see Chapter 5, page 78.

Coffee Break Water Closet

The Coffee Break is so called because, with a little luck, most of the materials needed to make it will be given to you in a café.

MATERIALS

Individual portion
  butter tubs (2)
Individual portion cream tub
Nozzle from hair dye
  container
Belthole eyelet
Three-strand necklace
  fastener
Bugle beads (2)
Balsa
Plastic straw
Bead
Chain
Necklace link

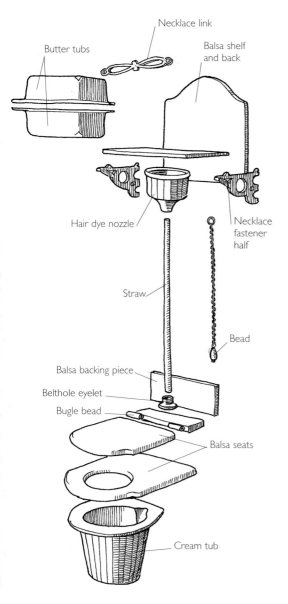

Necklace link

Butter tubs

Balsa shelf and back

Hair dye nozzle

Necklace fastener half

Straw

Bead

Balsa backing piece

Belthole eyelet

Bugle bead

Balsa seats

Cream tub

METHOD

1 Turn the cream tub so that the v-shaped lip is at the back.

2 Cut two seats from balsa and split the top seat at the back. Insert the bugle beads in the split for hinges, and glue the two seats together.

3 Glue the belthole eyelet to the centre back of the top seat to take the downpipe.

4 For the cistern, place the two butter tubs edge-to-edge, glue, and trim the edges. Shape a balsa back and shelf and stand the tubs on this. Add half the necklace fastener to each side for support brackets.

5 Attach a bead to one end of the chain and a necklace link to the other. Insert the link into the top of the cistern.

6 Glue the hair dye nozzle to the underside of the shelf. Cut the straw to length for the downpipe, glue one end into the nozzle and the other into the eyelet at the back of the toilet seat.

Sheila Blige's Flusher Toilet

Mona Bouttitt was rarely seen above stairs at Nearly Court, a house of ill-repute at the turn of the century. She didn't seem to appreciate what an honour it was to clean this magnificent piece of plumbing.

MATERIALS

Plastic roller ball from deodorant bottle
Firm card
Individual portion butter tubs (2)
Jump rings (2)
Chain
Small bead or solid chain link
Eye dropper nozzle
Three-strand necklace fastener
Brass foil
Balsa
Bugle beads (2)
Giftwrap
Long, solid link
Plastic straw
Stabilo Boss highlighter lid
Thin wire
Nut

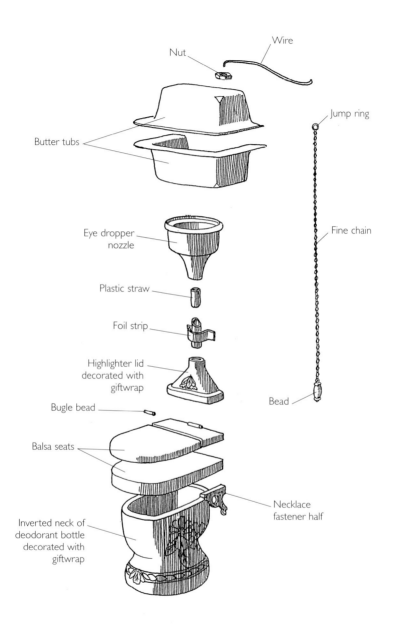

Nut

Wire

Butter tubs

Jump ring

Eye dropper nozzle

Fine chain

Plastic straw

Foil strip

Highlighter lid decorated with giftwrap

Bugle bead

Bead

Balsa seats

Necklace fastener half

Inverted neck of deodorant bottle decorated with giftwrap

METHOD

1 Remove the deodorant ball and cut across the top of the deodorant bottle to form the pedestal. Decorate it with flowers cut from giftwrap and coat with varnish.

2 Cut two seats from balsa and split the top seat at the back. Insert the bugle beads in this split for hinges. Glue the seats in place and disguise the join between the seat and the deodorant holder with a strip of firm card.

3 Support the pedestal with the necklace fastener, cut in two, one half on each side.

4 Cut the highlighter lid down, attach it to the back of the seat cover to take the down pipe, and decorate with a flower motif cut from giftwrap.

5 Place the two butter tubs together, edge-to-edge, glue and trim. Cut the back edge off the containers so that they sit flat against the wall. Glue the eye dropper nozzle underneath.

6 Pierce the cistern and insert a piece of bent wire. Disguise the join with a nut. Use the jump rings to attach a bead to one end of the chain, and the bent wire to the other.

7 Cut the straw to the required length and insert it between the cistern and the bowl. Place a strip of brass foil, bent to shape, across the pipe to fix it to the wall.

For details of loo roll holder, see Chapter 5, page 80.

25

Fruit Juice Opener Loo

When I open a carton of fruit juice, I'm struck how like a small toilet seat the plastic spout is. Seems a waste not to use it!

MATERIALS

Plastic aspirin bottle
Plastic spout from fruit
   juice carton
Plastic straw
Tiny metal ring
Necklace clasp
Individual portion butter tub
Small, flat bead or sequin
Belthole eyelet
Button
Balsa
Eye dropper nozzle
Chain
Bead
Paperclip

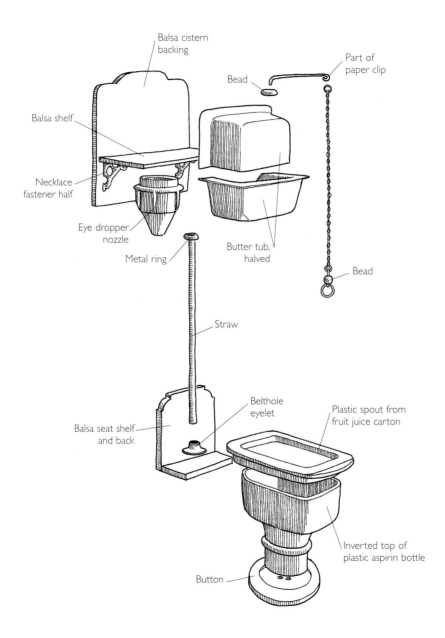

Balsa cistern backing

Bead

Part of paper clip

Balsa shelf

Necklace fastener half

Eye dropper nozzle

Metal ring

Butter tub, halved

Bead

Straw

Balsa seat shelf and back

Belthole eyelet

Plastic spout from fruit juice carton

Inverted top of plastic aspirin bottle

Button

METHOD

1   Cut the aspirin bottle off as shown. Remove the lid and replace it with a button. Paint both pieces white, and fit the fruit juice spout lid as the toilet seat.

2   Make up a balsa shelf and back to fit on the wall, and mount the loo on the shelf. Place the eyelet in the centre of the shelf to take the down-pipe.

3   Assemble the cistern by cutting the butter tub in half. Place one half on the other and trim the edges.

4   Make a balsa shelf to take the cistern and back it with a shaped balsa panel. Stand the cistern on the shelf and add a necklace clasp half to each side, under the shelf, for brackets. Pierce the cistern top and insert the flat bead or sequin and part of the paper clip, bent to shape. Attach another bead to one end of the chain and attach the other end of the chain to the paper-clip.

5   Fix the eye dropper nozzle under the cistern shelf. Trim the straw to size for the downpipe and fix a tiny metal ring to one end. Set the downpipe in position, with one end in the eyelet at the base and the other end in the nozzle.

For details of loo roll holder, brush and brush holder, see Chapter 5, pages 80 and 83.

The Old Bill

This is the only picture of one of the toilets removed by thieves in a dastardly raid on our local police station. Soon after the robbery, police issued a description of the missing toilets and added, 'at the moment we have nothing to go on'.

MATERIALS

Small metal egg cup
Balsa
Belthole eyelet
Foil card
Diamanté clip
Fine wire
Pins (2)
Cocktail stick
Solder or broad wire
Chain
Bead
Plastic straw
Long link
Bracelet link

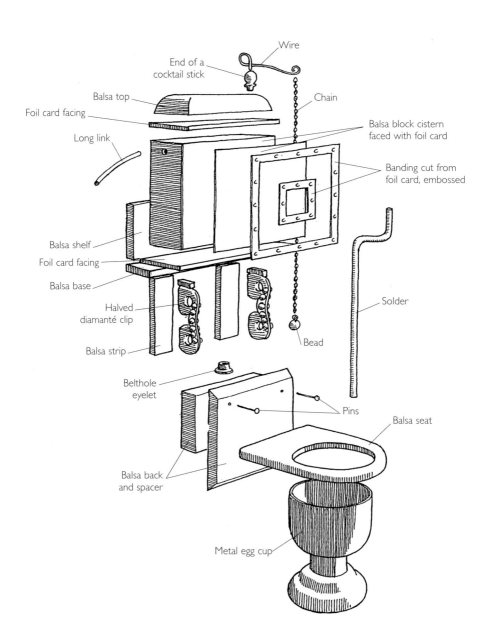

Wire

End of a
cocktail stick

Balsa top

Foil card facing

Long link

Chain

Balsa block cistern
faced with foil card

Banding cut from
foil card, embossed

Balsa shelf

Foil card facing

Balsa base

Halved
diamanté clip

Balsa strip

Solder

Bead

Belthole
eyelet

Pins

Balsa seat

Balsa back
and spacer

Metal egg cup

METHOD

1 Cut a block of balsa for the cistern. Face this block with panels cut from foil card. Cut strips of foil card and make indentations in the card side, with a needle or pin, to look like rivets on the foil side. Glue these strips to the front of the cistern.

2 Make a curved top for the cistern from balsa, filing it to shape, and add a balsa base. Paint the cistern assembly silver.

3 Cut the bracelet link in half and use these halves for the brackets below the cistern.

4 Cut the rounded end off a cocktail stick, then cut a groove into the top of this. Bend some fine wire to shape and fit one end of this wire into the groove. Sink the end of the cocktail stick into the top of the cistern at one side. Attach a bead to the chain and hang the chain from the free end of the wire.

5 Bend the long link as a soak-away pipe and insert it into the other side of the cistern.

6 Select a small egg cup and sink it into balsa wood. Cut an oval from the centre of this balsa to leave a toilet seat. (There's no lid on this model!) Cut a back support block from balsa, and another block to bring the loo away from the wall. File the balsa seat for comfort and neatness!

7 Mount the loo and stick pins in the back support to resemble screws.

8 Cut a length of solder for the downpipe and bend it to shape. Fix this solder in an eyelet and glue the eyelet behind the back support.

9 Make an L-shaped shelf from balsa to support the cistern. Glue the shelf and cistern assembly in place on the wall and add brackets, using halved diamanté clips glued to balsa strips. Fix the top of the downpipe into the base of the cistern.

For details of loo roll holder, see Chapter 5, page 80.

Housemaids' Slop Hopper

The philanthropic home for fallen women still has a few of these wonderful contraptions for washing out slops.

MATERIALS

TOILET
Opaque white vitamin
  pill tub
Eye dropper bottle cap
Balsa
Button *or* brooch
Rivets (2)
Solder
Cocktail fork
Oval shampoo bottle
Metal belt buckle
Chain
Bead
Jump ring
Foil card
Felt pen lid
Brass washer
Pins (2)
Brass-headed nail or pin

TAPS
Solder
Belthole eyelets (3)
Metal beads (2)
Press studs (2)
Pins (2)

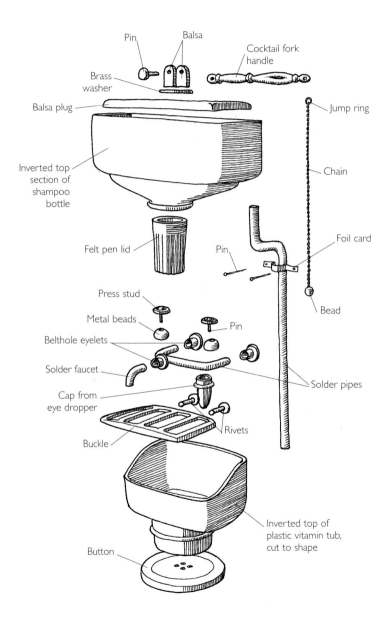

Pin

Balsa

Cocktail fork handle

Brass washer

Balsa plug

Jump ring

Inverted top section of shampoo bottle

Chain

Felt pen lid

Pin

Foil card

Press stud

Metal beads

Pin

Belthole eyelets

Solder faucet

Solder pipes

Bead

Cap from eye dropper

Buckle

Rivets

Inverted top of plastic vitamin tub, cut to shape

Button

METHOD

TOILET

1 Cut the vitamin tub to form a basin shape. Stand it upside down with its neck in a button or brooch. Fix the buckle to its back with two rivets so that its front rests on the lip of the basin. (The real ones lift up - yours will not!) Glue the eye dropper cap, upside down, to the back of the tub to take the downpipe.

2 Cut the top off the shampoo bottle then cut the screw thread off this to make a cistern. Make a hole in the felt pen lid to take the downpipe, and glue the lid into the hole from which the screw thread has been cut. Fill the open top of the cistern with a balsa plug. File the balsa to neaten it.

3 Stick a brass washer in the centre of the balsa lid. Round off the top of a small piece of balsa and cut a groove in this. Fit the handle end of a cocktail fork into this groove and fix in place with a brass-headed nail or pin. Attach a bead to one end of the chain, a jump ring to the other, and suspend from the fork.

4 Cut a length of solder for the downpipe and bend it to shape. Fit the top of the downpipe into the felt pen lid and the bottom into the cap on the tub. Cut a small sliver of foil card to bracket the downpipe to the wall, fixing it with the pins.

TAPS

1 Bend a small length of solder to give a wide 'u' shape and insert each end in an eyelet. Glue this length of solder across the downpipe.

2 Carefully bend another eyelet so that it will fit in the centre of the 'u' shape. Bend another piece of solder for a faucet and insert this into the bent eyelet.

3 For each tap, thread a bead, topped with a press stud, onto a pin. Glue these taps to the 'u' shape at either side of the downpipe, and cut off any pin that is showing.

For details of slop bucket, see Chapter 5, page 84.

The Hugh Vadditt Memorial W.C.

This loo is really fantasy, but I put it in to show what can be made from an unexpected find: in this case, a black plastic scent bottle top and lid.

MATERIALS

TOILET
Shaped black plastic nozzle
    and cap from a large
    scent bottle
Neck from a Stabilo
    Boss highlighter
Small pâté tub
Child's filigree hair comb
Stick-on furniture decoration
Long, blocked link
Jewellery findings (2)
Light card
Black drop earring
Dolls' house plastic railings
Tiny copper rings (2)
Chain
Bead
Copper pipe

LAMPS
Glass beads (2)
Bead caps (2)
Large metal beads (2)
Small, blocked bead caps (2)
Biro refill
Pins (4)
Small bead caps (2)
Small metal beads (2)

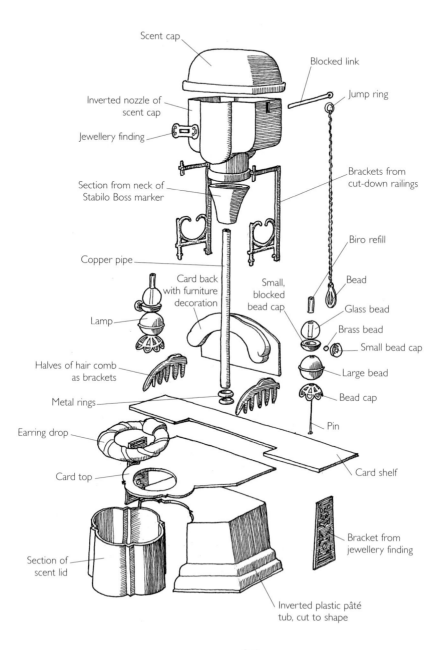

Scent cap

Blocked link

Jump ring

Inverted nozzle of
scent cap

Jewellery finding

Brackets from
cut-down railings

Section from neck of
Stabilo Boss marker

Biro refill

Copper pipe

Card back
with furniture
decoration

Small,
blocked
bead cap

Bead

Glass bead

Lamp

Brass bead

Small bead cap

Halves of hair comb
as brackets

Large bead

Metal rings

Bead cap

Earring drop

Pin

Card top

Card shelf

Section of
scent lid

Bracket from
jewellery finding

Inverted plastic pâté
tub, cut to shape

METHOD

TOILET

1 Cut the end off the pâté tub and use it, upside down, for the loo base. Cut a hole in the front of the base to take the scent lid. Glue the lid in place. Top the whole of the loo seat with card, cut to shape. Fix an earring drop on top of the card for the toilet lid, leaving space at the back for the downpipe.

2 Add a card shelf across the back, supported by brackets made from jewellery findings, cut in half. Add a second pair of brackets, made from a hair comb cut in half, to the top of the shelf, at either side of the bowl. Spray paint the base assembly.

3 Back the toilet bowl with a shaped piece of card, also painted black, and top this with a furniture decoration.

4 Cut the copper pipe to size for the downpipe. Fit it into the rings and attach it at the back of the bowl.

5 Remove the spray tube from the scent nozzle and turn the nozzle upside down. Whittle the neck from the Stabilo Boss highlighter to fit it into the scent nozzle and fix the copper pipe into the other end of the neck. Use the rounded scent cap as a cistern lid. Stick a jewellery finding, as a maker's nameplate, at the front of the cistern.
Support the cistern with brackets made from cut-down railings.

6 Attach a bead to one end of the chain and a blocked link to the other, using jump rings if needed. Bore a hole in the side of the cistern and hang the blocked link from this.

LAMPS

1 For each lamp, thread onto a pin in the following order: a bead cap (upside down), a large bead, a small, blocked bead cap, a glass bead, and a tiny length of biro refill (the clear section from the top). Glue the pieces together and withdraw the pin.

2 Again for each lamp, insert a pin through a small bead cap and a brass bead, snip off any excess length of pin, and glue the assembly to the side of the lamp, below the glass bead.

The Royale (a throne fit for a king)

Popular throughout the length and breadth of the kingdom, especially in palaces and stately homes where the ruling classes need the tranquillity to sit and make important decisions. A broken toy roundabout was the inspiration for this model – that's where I found the sconce on which I mounted the cistern.

MATERIALS

Sconce *or* rectangular brooch
    or chain belt lozenge
Small oval lid *or* pot
Sturdy filigree links from
    chain belt
Light filigree bracelet
Flower-shaped brooch
    mounting
Embossed trimming
Metal nut
Blocked link
Balsa
Chain
Bead
Cartridge case, .22
Screw eyelet
Copper pipe
Copper foil
Light card
Bugle beads (2)
Shampoo nozzle

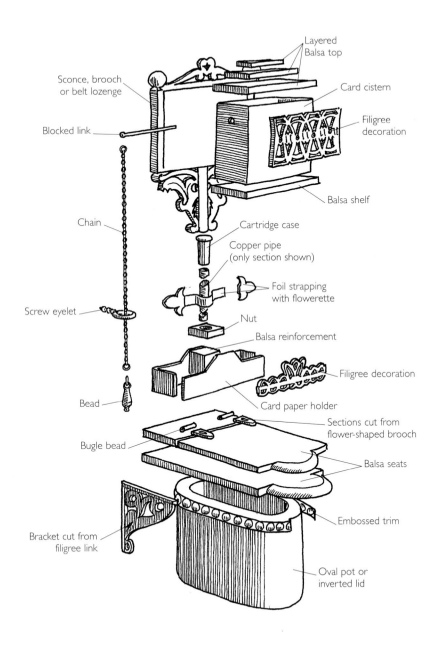

Layered Balsa top

Sconce, brooch or belt lozenge

Card cistern

Filigree decoration

Blocked link

Balsa shelf

Chain

Cartridge case

Copper pipe (only section shown)

Foil strapping with flowerette

Screw eyelet

Nut

Balsa reinforcement

Filigree decoration

Card paper holder

Bead

Sections cut from flower-shaped brooch

Bugle bead

Balsa seats

Embossed trim

Bracket cut from filigree link

Oval pot or inverted lid

METHOD

1 Use an oval lid or pot for the base and bind the top of this with embossed trimming.

2 Cut two seats from balsa, making the top one slightly smaller than the lower one. Make a split across the back of the top seat and insert the two bugle beads in the split, then add small sections cut from the flower-shaped brooch mounting to make fancy hinges.

3 Make up the paper holder in light card, score and bend it to form a box. Glue the box to hold it together and reinforce the centre with balsa. Top the centre of the box with a nut to take the down-pipe. Attach the paper holder to the back of the seat and paint the whole assembly brown. Decorate the box with a filigree bracelet link.

4 Add filigree findings to either side of the loo bowl, for brackets.

5 Make a box for the cistern from card, layer balsa at the top and add a shelf at the bottom of it. Mount the cistern on a sconce, brooch or belt lozenge. (My sconce had a down piece incorporated – if yours doesn't, add a shampoo nozzle to take the downpipe.) Paint the cistern assembly brown and decorate the front with a filigree chain belt link.

6 Fix the cartridge case to the down piece. (This is not necessary if you have used a shampoo nozzle.) Cut a length of copper pipe and seat it in the nut at the base and in the cartridge case or shampoo nozzle at the top. Bracket the pipe to the wall with a strip of copper foil bent to shape, finished with flowerettes cut from brooch mounting.

7 Attach the chain to the bead at one end and the blocked link at the other, and insert the free end of the link into the side of the cistern.

8 Fix the screw eyelet to the wall and pass the chain through the eyelet.

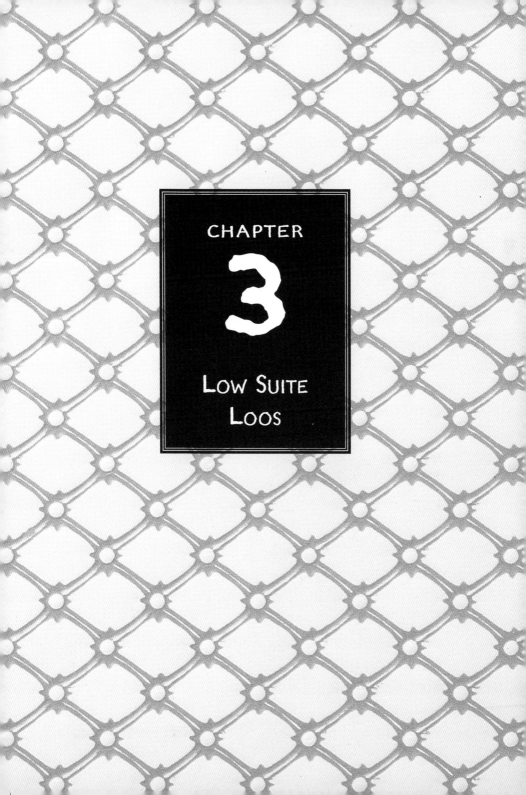

CHAPTER

3

LOW SUITE LOOS

The Sylvan Glade Low Suite Floral W.C.

If you have never used a deodorant egg in your fridge, now is the time to start, because the bubble pack it comes in is perfect for a 1/12 scale toilet pan.

METHOD

1 Cut off the base of the lolly mould and use this, rim side down, for the pedestal base. Cut the rounded part off the bubble pack and keep the shaped half. Attach this shaped part to the lolly mould. Paint the whole assembly white.

2 Carefully cut suitable patterns and flowers from paper and glue them inside and outside both the bowl and the pedestal. Varnish to keep the patterns in place.

3 Cut and stain a balsa seat and glue it to the bowl. Add furniture decorations for brackets.

4 Make and panel a small card box for a cistern, and cut a card top and a balsa base and top. The balsa top for the cistern should slightly protrude at the front. Add card panelling to the front and glue the cistern in place. Finish the cistern with part of a brooch finding mounted in a plain bead cap.

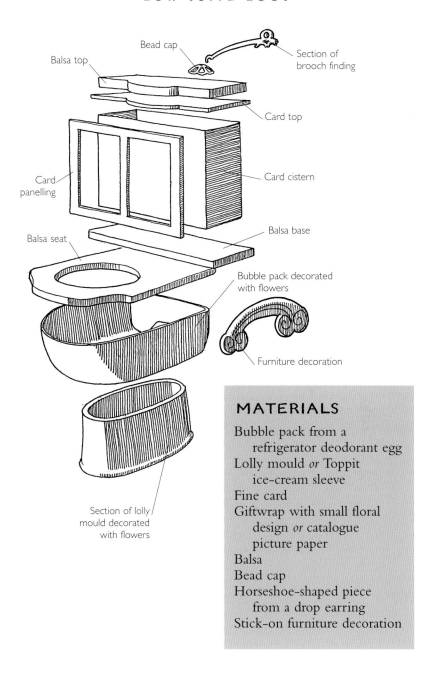

Bead cap

Balsa top

Section of
brooch finding

Card top

Card
panelling

Card cistern

Balsa seat

Balsa base

Bubble pack decorated
with flowers

Furniture decoration

Section of lolly
mould decorated
with flowers

MATERIALS

Bubble pack from a
refrigerator deodorant egg

Lolly mould *or* Toppit
ice-cream sleeve

Fine card

Giftwrap with small floral
design *or* catalogue
picture paper

Balsa

Bead cap

Horseshoe-shaped piece
from a drop earring

Stick-on furniture decoration

The Blue Rose Low Suite

I met an electrician recently who had rescued one of these from the sledge hammer, and having nowhere else to sit, the pedestal now resides below the unit in his kitchen - and very nice it looks! 'I'm saving it for posterity', he told me, and I was proud to know him.

MATERIALS

Lolly mould
Bugle beads (2)
Inside tube from a plastic
    hypodermic needle
Toothbrush holder
Fimo
Kinder egg ($\frac{1}{2}$)
Floral giftwrap
Belthole eyelet
Long, blocked link
Chain
Bead
Balsa
Eyedropper nozzle

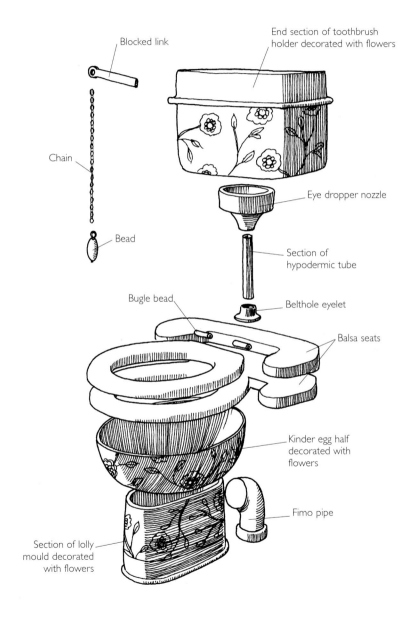

Blocked link

End section of toothbrush holder decorated with flowers

Chain

Eye dropper nozzle

Bead

Section of hypodermic tube

Bugle bead

Belthole eyelet

Balsa seats

Kinder egg half decorated with flowers

Fimo pipe

Section of lolly mould decorated with flowers

METHOD

1 Cut the lolly mould to the height required for the pedestal. Glue the half egg (cut lengthwise) to this pedestal, to make the bowl. Decorate the bowl and pedestal, inside and out, with flowers cut from giftwrap. Varnish the flowers to fix them. Mould a waste pipe from Fimo.

2 Cut and stain two balsa seats. Fix the lower one in place. Split the top seat and insert two bugle beads in the split to represent hinges. Place the belthole eyelet in the centre back of the upper seat to take the downpipe.

3 For the cistern, cut the end off the toothbrush holder, through the top and bottom. Glue the top to the bottom and add floral decoration. Fix the eyedropper nozzle to the base of the cistern. Pierce the side of the cistern and insert the blocked link. Attach a bead to one end of the chain, and hang the other end from the blocked link.

4 Cut the hypodermic tube to length for a downpipe. Insert the downpipe into the eyelet on the seat assembly and fix the other end to the eyedropper nozzle.

46

Thoroughly Modern Mini

Streamlined stuff is not much fun to model as there are no twiddly bits to liven it up, and this model might never have seen the light of day had not my eye been taken by the oval hair conditioner bottle with a loo-seat-shaped lid – obviously sold with miniature modellers in mind. While I was in the chemists I was able to pick up a couple of extra aids to modelling: now the family are squeaky-clean and we have a new model as well.

MATERIALS

Touch of Silk hair
    conditioner lid
Boots intensive care hand
    lotion bottle
Artificial sweetener
    handbag pack
Hanging shower gel top
Earring drop
Bead cap
Pin
Balsa

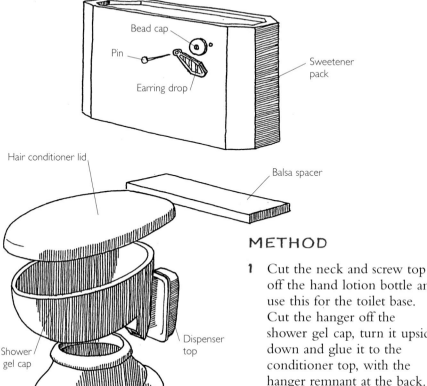

Bead cap

Pin

Earring drop

Sweetener pack

Hair conditioner lid

Balsa spacer

Shower gel cap

Dispenser top

Bottle neck and top

METHOD

1 Cut the neck and screw top off the hand lotion bottle and use this for the toilet base. Cut the hanger off the shower gel cap, turn it upside down and glue it to the conditioner top, with the hanger remnant at the back. Cover this with the dispenser top from the sweetener pack. Use the conditioner lid for the toilet seat cover. Mount the whole assembly slightly out from the wall, using a balsa spacer, to leave room for the cistern.

2 Use the sweetener pack for the cistern. Pass a pin through the earring drop and bead cap and insert it into the cistern.

British Raj Thunderbox

Property of Major Rodeahead, late (and he always was!) of the Veripaur Lancers. In the days of the British Raj, army officers were in the habit of taking their own portable water closets wherever they went (if you see what I mean).

MATERIALS

Firm card
Individual portion cream tub
Filigree links from a
    chain belt
Balsa
Brass washer
Jewellery finding
Horseshoe-shaped piece
    from drop earring

METHOD

1 Cut balsa to a rectangle for
the base of the box. Score the
length of card to bend it and
make a box around the base.
Glue the balsa floor into it.
Cut a second rectangle of
balsa slightly larger than the
first. Stand the box on the
larger base and glue it in
place.

2 Decorate the front of the box
with filigree links and cut
strips of card to make
panelling around them.
Use light card to make a top
for the box, and cut a circular
hole in it to take the cream
tub. Do not assemble yet!

3 Place a strip of balsa at the
back of the box, along its
length. Cut a second top,
from balsa, and then cut this
into three pieces as illustrated,
one with a hole cut from it
for the seat cover.

4 Make an 'all over' lid from
two rectangles of balsa, one
larger than the other, glued
together.

5 Spray paint all the parts
except the tub and 'brass'
pieces. When dry, glue the
tub in place and reassemble
the loo with the lids up.

6 Attach two jewellery findings
to the lid for hinges.

7 Fix the brass washer and
horseshoe-shaped earring
piece in place for a handle.

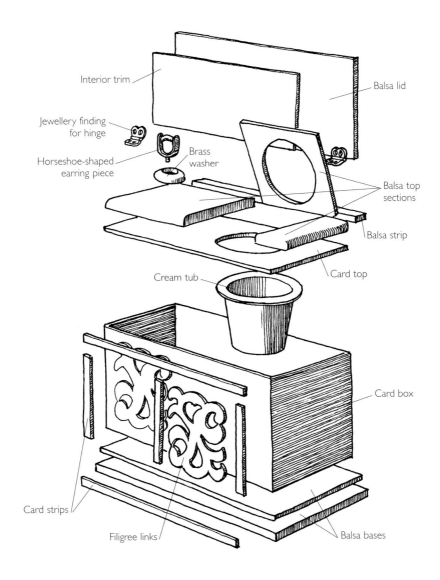

Interior trim

Balsa lid

Jewellery finding
for hinge

Horseshoe-shaped
earring piece

Brass
washer

Balsa top
sections

Balsa strip

Cream tub

Card top

Card box

Card strips

Filigree links

Balsa bases

Sitting Pretty Comfy Commode

When she came to live in my dolls' house, the memsahib retired to her bed suffering, she said, from bouts of malaria (I suspected gin). She demanded I make her a comfy commode in a hurry and was much relieved when I complied.

MATERIALS

Medium card
Beads (4)
Balsa
Filigree metal
    bracelet links (2)
McDonald's
    stirring spoons (2)
Fabric scrap
Individual portion cream tub
Buckle ($\frac{1}{2}$)

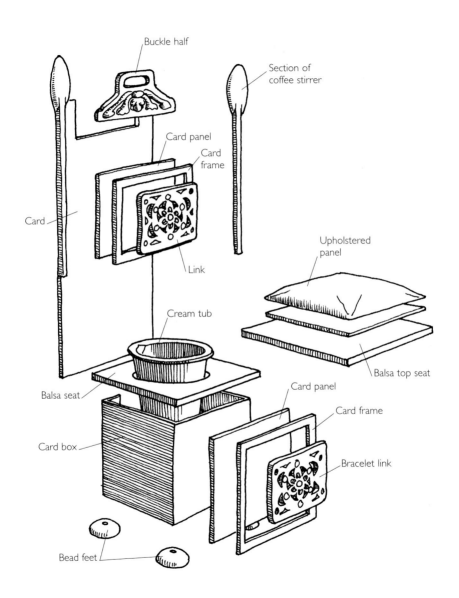

Buckle half

Section of
coffee stirrer

Card panel

Card
frame

Card

Link

Upholstered
panel

Cream tub

Balsa top seat

Balsa seat

Card panel

Card frame

Card box

Bracelet link

Bead feet

53

METHOD

1 Make up a card box for the chair base. Top this with a balsa seat, cutting a central hole. Trim the cream tub and place it in the hole. Cut a front panel, glue a bracelet link in the centre and frame this with card. Decorate the front of the chair base with this panel.

2 Cut a back for the chair from card, using half a buckle for a top rung. Cut an extra panel and decorate it with a framed link. Attach this to the chair back. Glue a stirrer, cut to length, at either side of the chair back, and fix the back to the base.

3 Cut a top seat from balsa, to protrude slightly.

4 Spray paint the whole chair brown.

5 Upholster a smaller panel and glue it to the centre of the balsa seat. Attach the seat to the chair, and raise the whole chair on four bead feet.

CHAPTER

4

OUTDOOR AND
PUBLIC LOOS

The Willoughby Long High St Urinal

These lovely wrought-iron fixtures used to be seen in almost every High street. Now they are gone – more's the pity – so, in loving memory...

MATERIALS

BUILDING
Fancy picture frame, about
    4 x 6in (10 x 15cm)
Embossed metallic cake
    frill strip
Filigree links from chain
    belt (10)
Stick-on furniture moulding
Firm card
Dowel
Cocktail stick
Long brooch
Snap fasteners
Rawlplug

LAMP AND BRACKET
Hand-held mirror handle
Scroll holder from pet's
    name tag
Kinder egg ($^1/_2$)
Round brooch finding
Button (to fit brooch
    finding)
Metal button *or*
    keyhole cover
Chain
Plastic cup handle
Wire
Jump ring

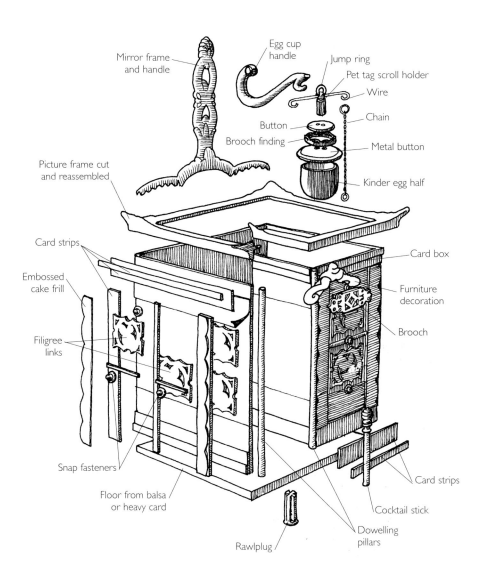

Mirror frame
and handle

Egg cup
handle

Jump ring

Pet tag scroll holder

Wire

Chain

Button

Brooch finding

Metal button

Kinder egg half

Picture frame cut
and reassembled

Card strips

Card box

Embossed
cake frill

Furniture
decoration

Brooch

Filigree
links

Snap fasteners

Card strips

Floor from balsa
or heavy card

Cocktail stick

Dowelling
pillars

Rawlplug

57

METHOD

BUILDING

1   Cut enough card for the whole building, to the required height. Score the card and bend it to form a box that will fit below the picture frame. Score the front of the box and bend part of the wall inwards to make the entrance.

2   Cut the front of the frame and reassemble to make a cornice to fit the entrance. Glue the frame to the top of the card box.

3   Cut a floor and glue it in place. Reinforce the doorway with dowelling pillars and add a cocktail stick handle as a bollard. Use a brooch and stick-on furniture decoration to make an arch for the entrance, and fix it in place.

4   Bind the base and top of the urinal with thin strips of card, scored to give neat corners. Decorate the urinal with strips of embossed cake frill, and add filigree links to complete the decorative panels. Use snap fasteners for extra detail.

5   Fix the rawlplug by the door for a post.

6   Spray paint the whole building.

LAMP AND BRACKET

1   Use the half Kinder egg as the light, and mount this to hang under the metal button. Top the button with a brooch finding, and fill it with a button to fit. Glue the pet tag scroll holder above this to top off the lamp. Thread a wire through the hole in the scroll holder, curl the wire at each end and attach a length of chain at each side of the lamp.

2   Remove the mirror from its frame and cut the frame to give short lengths at either side of the handle. Bend the frame to fit along the back of the urinal, at the top. Glue in place and add the cup handle as a light bracket. Hang the lamp from the handle with a jump ring.

Ladies' Municipal Toilet

This whole enterprise was inspired by the find of an old 45-type record rack: cut in half it made two roofs, and what better to do with them than make two municipal W.C.s!

MATERIALS

Plastic record rack
Card
Individual portion
    cream tubs (2)
Blocked links (2)
Small picture frame
Wooden moulding strips
Balsa
Solder wire
Beads (2)
Chain
Jewellery finding
Foamcore *or* featherboard
Turned banister rods
Giftwrap
Haze room freshener
    container
Gold beads
Black map pins

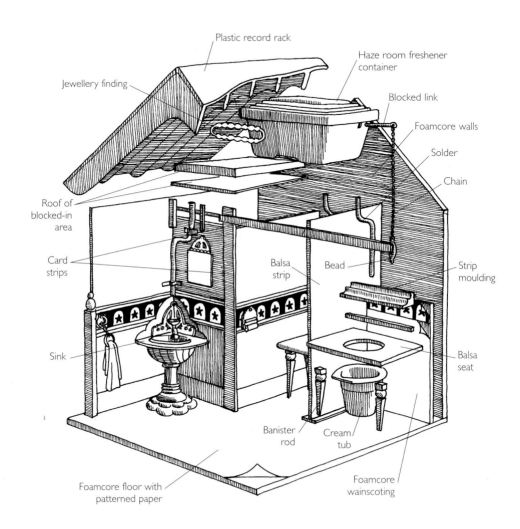

Plastic record rack

Haze room freshener container

Jewellery finding

Blocked link

Foamcore walls

Solder

Chain

Roof of blocked-in area

Card strips

Balsa strip

Bead

Strip moulding

Sink

Balsa seat

Banister rod

Cream tub

Foamcore floor with patterned paper

Foamcore wainscoting

METHOD

1 Cut the record rack in half. Use one piece, upside down, for the roof, and make three walls from foamcore to hold the roof. Do not glue the roof in place until you have completed the interior details. Divide the available space into stalls with balsa strips, blocking in one corner up to the washbasin area. I used a small picture frame for the roof of this blocked-in section.

2 Add a layer of foamcore to the walls for wainscoting, then paper and panel the walls and floor, using strip moulding for effect. Add finials to the dividing walls by passing map pins through gold beads (shown in photo only).

3 Cut balsa seats to fit across the stalls. Trace around the cream tubs and cut holes in the seats a little smaller than the drawn circles. Place a tub under each hole and glue them into position. Add legs (banister rods) to the front of the seats only, and glue the seat backs to the wainscoting.

4 Construct door frames for the stalls.

5 For the cistern, fix the Haze container between the stalls, centrally, and decorate it with a jewellery finding. Bend two lengths of solder for the downpipes. Glue one end of each to the cistern, and the other end to the wainscoting. Insert a blocked link on either side of the cistern. Hang a length of chain, complete with a bead, from each cistern.

6 Glue the roof in place.

For details of washbasin, see Chapter 5, page 86.

Gentlemen's Municipal Urinal

You will need a fair amount of gall to explain to the average art shop assistant why you need the packaging oil paint tubes come in, but that over, the rest is easy, and it gives a whole new meaning to the phrase 'down the tubes'!

MATERIALS

Foamcore
Wood strip
Clear plastic record rack
Giftwrap
'Six-pack' oil paint packaging
Haze room freshener
    container
Brass nut
Tiny metal ring
Nozzle from tiny
    eyedrop bottle
Solder wire *or* wire
Long, rectangular Tupperware
    or other plastic storage lid

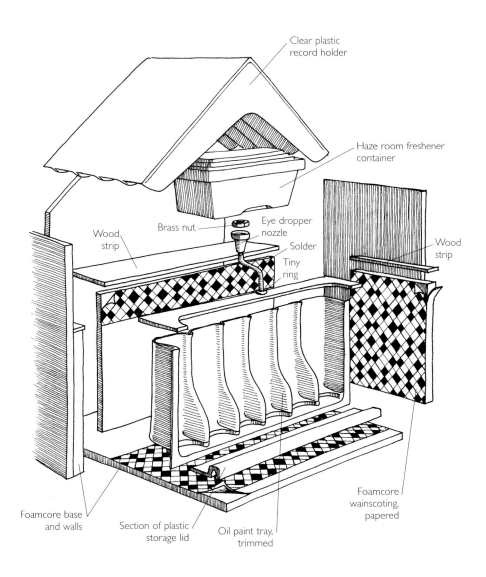

Clear plastic
record holder

Haze room freshener
container

Wood
strip

Brass nut

Eye dropper
nozzle

Solder

Tiny
ring

Wood
strip

Foamcore base
and walls

Section of plastic
storage lid

Oil paint tray,
trimmed

Foamcore
wainscoting,
papered

METHOD

1 Cut the record rack in half. Use one half as the roof, and cut three walls from foamcore to fit it.

2 Trim the oil paint tray to look like a urinal (take off the top and bottom), then cut it to fit across the width of the room. Fix the tiny ring in place in the centre of the urinal, at the top.

3 Construct wainscoting from foamcore so that it is just below the height of the urinal on the side walls and a little higher than the urinal on the back wall. Paper the wainscoting and floor, and glue the urinal in place. Top the wainscoting on the side and back walls with the wood strip.

4 Remove the lip along one side of the storage lid and use it for the soakaway, trimming it to fit. Glue it in place in front of the stalls.

5 Use the Haze container for the cistern. Glue it shut and cut the back off so that it is not too deep. Place the nut in the centre, underneath. Cut the eyedropper nozzle down and attach it to the nut to take the downpipe. Bend the solder wire to shape for the downpipe, and attach it to the nozzle at one end and the tiny ring at the other.

6 Spray the cistern silver with a light overspray of black.

For details of mop bucket and washbasin, see Chapter 5, pages 85 and 88.

The Twin-Pack Urinal

It's all your fault if I am no longer the trim size 12 that I once was. I have sacrificed my sylph-like figure in an endless search on your behalf and, try as I may, I have found nothing so satisfactory for this model as a bubble pack which contained two chocolate éclairs . . . and, of course, I needed to have several attempts, so several packs, to get it right!

MATERIALS

Bubble pack for two éclairs
Plastic lens bubble packs (2)
Press studs (4)
Belthole eyelets (5)
Individual portion butter tub
Plastic tea stirrers (2)
Bowl-shaped earring
Solder *or* metal tube
Metal nuts (2)
Rectangular bean slicer
Card
Beads (3)

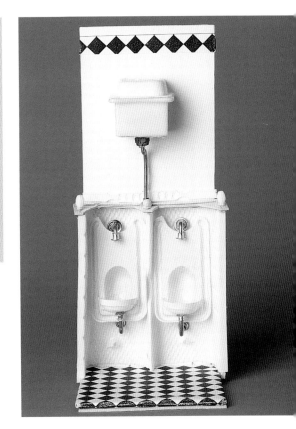

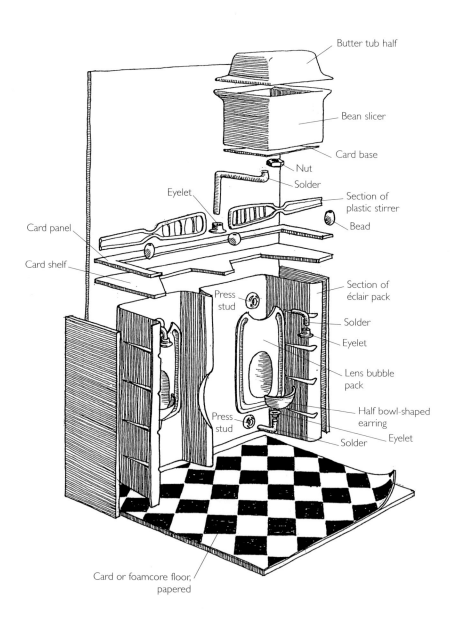

Butter tub half

Bean slicer

Card base

Nut

Solder

Eyelet

Section of
plastic stirrer

Bead

Card panel

Card shelf

Press
stud

Section of
éclair pack

Solder

Eyelet

Lens bubble
pack

Press
stud

Half bowl-shaped
earring

Eyelet

Solder

Card or foamcore floor,
papered

METHOD

1 Cut the rounded top and bottom ends off the éclair pack. Stand the cut pack on card and draw around the base. Using this outline, cut a shelf to go above the éclair pack to disguise the top. Glue the pack to the wall and floor, and add the shelf to the top. Add a further card panel to the shelf and decorate the wall above the shelf with stirrers cut to size.

2 Glue a lens pack into each stall. Cut the bowl-shaped earring in half to make a basin under each lens pack. Make entry pipes out of bent solder mounted on a press stud, each with an eyelet as a spout. Make exit pipes in the same way.

3 Fix a belthole eyelet in the centre of the top shelf, to house the downpipe, and fix three beads across the top of the shelf.

4 Use the bean slicer, topped with half a butter tub, for the cistern, add a card base and glue a nut underneath. Bend solder to shape for the downpipe, and fix in place.

The P. King Chinese Takeaway Loo

Clock cases make very good settings for dolls' house scenes and I always keep a lookout for them. I had in mind something in dark oak when I saw a plastic, pagoda-style clock in such faultless bad taste, I felt it deserved some special treatment – the Chinese takeaway loo was the result.

MATERIALS

Plastic pagoda-style clock case
Card
Shaped stripwood
Louvred packing from box
    of chocolates
Plastic filigree fan
Tiny drop earrings (pair)
Nozzle from a hair
    colourant tube
Individual portion
    butter tubs (2)
Giftwrap, Chinese-style
    and plain
Metal nut *or* belthole eyelet
Cake pillar
Child's plastic hair comb
Chain
Bead
Solder
Large drop earring
Long blocked link
Individual portion jam tub
Balsa

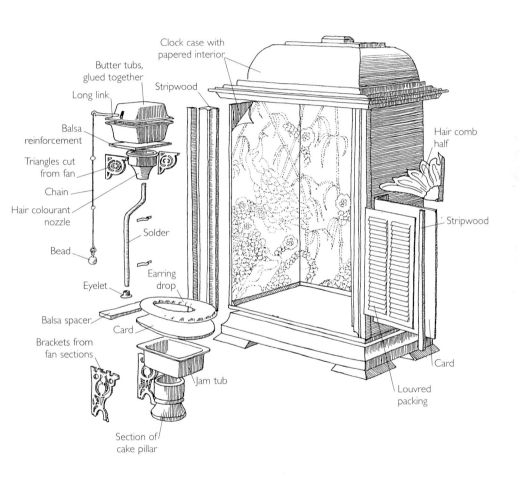

Clock case with papered interior

Butter tubs, glued together

Stripwood

Long link

Balsa reinforcement

Hair comb half

Triangles cut from fan

Chain

Hair colourant nozzle

Solder

Stripwood

Bead

Earring drop

Eyelet

Balsa spacer

Card

Card

Brackets from fan sections

Louvred packing

Jam tub

Section of cake pillar

METHOD

1   Remove the clock mechanism from the box in which it is housed. Keep the lid and the base, but if the box itself is not high enough for your purposes, replace it with a custom-made box. Fill in both sides with stripwood. (These strips will support the doors). Paper the interior with the Chinese-style giftwrap, and paper the floor.

2   Cut the cake pillar to height and top with the jam tub. Trim the edges to neaten. Use an earring drop for the loo seat cover: trace around it onto card, cut the card shape out and mount the earring on it. Spray the seat brown. When dry, glue the seat cover onto the jam tub to complete the pedestal unit.

3   Cut two lengths of fan for brackets. Remove the front edge from these and trim to shape. Add a sliver of balsa behind the pedestal to bring it into view. Glue the pedestal and brackets in place.

4   Shape the solder to make a downpipe. Insert the top into the hair colourant nozzle and

the bottom into a nut or eyelet. (The length of solder will have to be adjusted later).

5   Glue two butter tubs together face-to-face, and trim to neaten. Reinforce this cistern with a square of balsa underneath. Attach the downpipe to the cistern and the pedestal, adjusting the length as necessary, and fix the cistern to the wall. Shape triangles cut from the fan as brackets for the cistern. Attach a length of chain ending in a bead to a long link. Pierce the cistern and insert the end of the long link for a chain pull.

6   Cut two pieces of card for the doors and score each to give a 'hinge'. Reinforce these with stripwood, add louvres, and top each door with half a hair comb. Pierce a hole in each to take the handles, made of tiny drop earrings attached with pins.

For details of washbasin, see Chapter 5, page 91.

70

Think Tank: Outside Shed

It is possible this was not in Greta Garbo's mind when she uttered the immortal words 'I want to be alone', nevertheless, it is often the only place lesser mortals can be guaranteed privacy.

MATERIALS

Foamcore
Medium card
Balsa
Individual portion cream tub

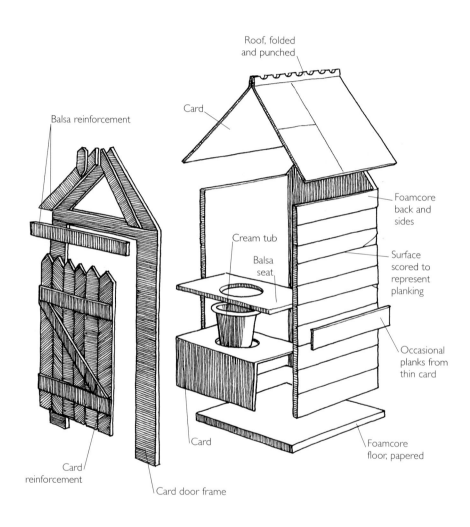

Roof, folded
and punched

Card

Balsa reinforcement

Cream tub

Balsa
seat

Foamcore
back and
sides

Surface
scored to
represent
planking

Occasional
planks from
thin card

Card
reinforcement

Card

Card door frame

Foamcore
floor, papered

METHOD

1   Cut out the back and sides from foamcore, in one piece. Score along the dotted lines and bend the sides forward.

2   Cut the roof, front and door pieces from card. To create a plank effect for the walls, score horizontal lines and add an occasional layer of card to some planks while peeling the top layer off others to give variety, and chamfer off a few corners to give a weathered look.

3   Cut out a triangle above the door, and reinforce with balsa 'beams'. Score door panels and add reinforcing planks in a reverse 'Z' on the outside.

4   Make the walls and door up into a house and add a floor of foamcore, papering it before you put it in place.

5   Cut out a card seat unit, score and bend, then cut out a balsa seat to top this. Trace around the cream tub on the centre of both these pieces, and then cut around the tracing. Position the cream tub under the seat unit and top with the balsa seat. Glue the whole assembly together, and fix it in position in the hut. If you want to neaten the assembly, run a strip of balsa along the back of the seat unit, as shown in the photo.

6   Score the roof and bend it so there is a ridge in the centre. Cut 'bites' out of this ridge at regular intervals, with a leather punch. Score lines on the roof to represent tar paper panels. Lift the corner of one to give a worn look.

7   Paint the interior, then glue on the roof. Set the whole thing on a base of balsa and decorate with twigs, lichens and perhaps a flower pot!

For details of loo paper holder, see Chapter 5, page 81.

Tinklebell Authentic Fairy's Toilet

This is something of an exclusive! In my research for authenticity I have left no stone unturned. Indeed, it was under one stone that a hitherto undiscovered fairy's toilet came to light, thus disproving the widely-held Victorian myth that fairies never did anything of the sort!

MATERIALS

Card
Balsa
Walnut (½)
Wooden chesspiece
Tiny chain
Bamboo tablemat (optional)
Bead
Long bracelet link
Stones
Twigs
Dried leaves
Shells
Grasses
Giftwrap
Dried gourd *or* coconut shell
Poppy head *or* snail's shell
White plastic straw
Washers *or* eyelets (2)
Bugle beads (2)
Commercial hook for
    front-opening dolls' house
Ring
Kitchen paper

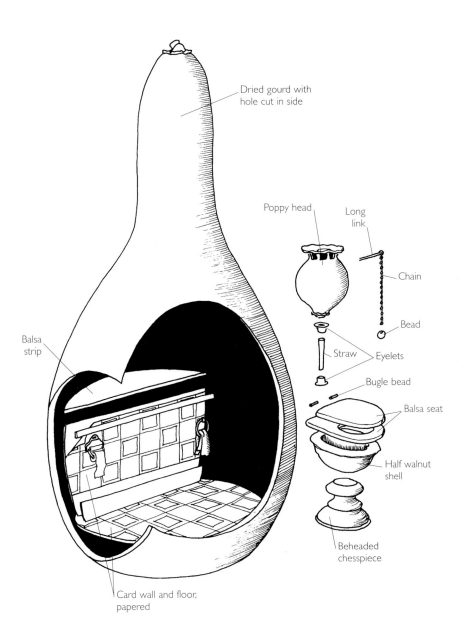

Dried gourd with hole cut in side

Poppy head

Long link

Chain

Bead

Eyelets

Straw

Bugle bead

Balsa seat

Half walnut shell

Beheaded chesspiece

Balsa strip

Card wall and floor, papered

METHOD

1 To gain height and avoid all the other problems you encounter when you try to furnish a rounded object, use card to fit a small retaining wall and add a false floor to make a flat base (there is nothing so upsetting as a wonky loo!), but do not fix these in place yet.

2 Mark on the outside of the gourd where you want the opening to be and pierce a series of small holes around its circumference. This makes it easy to cut from hole to hole with a craft knife and remove the panel. (Either keep the panel to use as a door, or use the bamboo tablemat.) Hollow out and tidy the interior and paint it white.

3 Paper the floor and wall, and finish the wall with a balsa strip top. Glue the floor and wall in place.

4 Use half a walnut for the loo bowl, and top it with a balsa seat and lid. Split the lid at the back and insert two bugle beads for hinges. Glue the seat assembly to a beheaded chesspiece.

5 A poppy head forms the cistern. Bore a hole in its base and a tiny hole in its side and insert an eyelet into the base of the poppy head. Into the eyelet glue a straw cut to the length you want. Slip the base of the straw into another eyelet and attach it to the loo as a downpipe. Hang a bead on a length of chain and attach the top of it to a long link. Insert one end of this link into the hole in the poppy head's side.

6 Glue the loo roll holder to the wall, within easy reach of the seat. Mount a ring, with a towel made of kitchen paper, on the wall.

7 Add a door, using either the cut-out panel or part of a bamboo tablemat, held open with a metal hook.

8 Camouflage with the leaves, shells, twigs and stones.

For details of loo roll holder and washbasin, see Chapter 5, pages 78 and 90.

CHAPTER

5

FIXTURES AND
FITTINGS

Loo Roll Holders

DIAMANTÉ CLIP

MATERIALS

Diamanté clip
Straw
Paper

Diamanté clip

Straw

METHOD

Diamanté clips already have a bar across them so to convert them to a loo roll holder, all you have to do is cut across a length of straw so that you can push it over the existing bar, then wind a length of paper around it!

From The Goliath, page 18

BRACELET LINK

MATERIALS

Straw
Bracelet link
Wire
Paper

METHOD

Use a small piece of straw for the toilet roll, wrap paper around it, and wire this onto a bracelet link.

Bracelet link

Wire

Paper wound around straw

From Tinklebell Authentic Fairy's Toilet, page 74

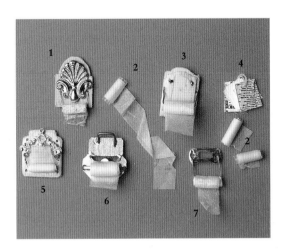

1   Earring finding on shaped balsa
2   Paper wrapped around straw
3   Wire on balsa
    (*from The Old Bill*)
4   Silko (*from Think Tank*)
5   Necklace fastener
    (*from Fruit Juice Opener Loo*)
6   Trouser fly bar
    (*rustic version of Diamanté Clip,*
    from The Goliath)
7   Bracelet link
    (*from Tinklebell Authentic*
    Fairy's Toilet)

NECKLACE FASTENER

MATERIALS

Straw
Paper
Wire
Necklace fastener
Balsa

METHOD

For the loo roll, wind paper around a length of straw. Wire this to a necklace fastener and back the fastener with a shaped piece of balsa. For a more rustic version, omit the necklace fastener and wire the straw straight into the balsa.

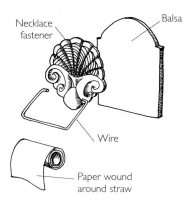

Necklace fastener

Balsa

Wire

Paper wound around straw

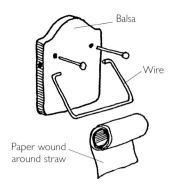

Balsa

Wire

Paper wound around straw

From Sheila Blige's Flusher Toilet, page 23;
Fruit Juice Opener Loo, page 26;
The Old Bill (rustic version), page 29

SILKO

MATERIALS

Small newspaper adverts
    and clippings
Silko
Pin

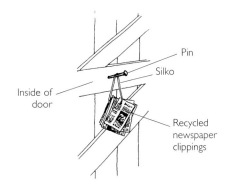

METHOD

Reduce the adverts and clippings by photocopying. Hang a wodge of
the cut papers on a length of Silko and hook it over a pin stuck to the
inside of the door.

From Think Tank: Outside Shed, page 71

EXTRA LOO ROLL HOLDERS

All sorts of findings, clips and fobs can be used for loo roll holders. Wind a strip of paper around a short piece of drinking straw and wire it to a key fob. Use a trouser fly catch bar to take the paper and glue it to a handbag fastener. Thread the toilet roll on part of a watchstrap bar and glue it to a drop earring. Wire a roll of paper below a drop earring and mount the earring on a shaped piece of balsa . . .

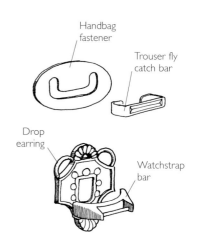

Handbag fastener

Trouser fly catch bar

Drop earring

Watchstrap bar

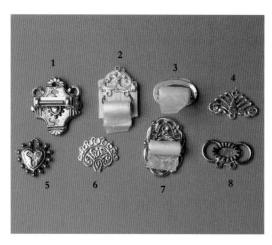

1 Key fob with bar from watch case
2 Necklace fastener
3 Part of handbag clasp
4 Necklace clasp
5 Tiny pendant
6 Jewellery finding
7 Link from bracelet
8 Necklace clasp

Brushes and Buckets

BRUSH AND BRUSH HOLDER

MATERIALS

Mascara wand *or* brush
    from a hair curler and
    cocktail stick
Small cartridge

METHOD

Use the cartridge for the brush
holder, and cut down the mascara
wand to size for the brush. If you
are using a hair curler for the
brush, use a turned cocktail stick
for the handle.

From Fruit Juice Opener Loo, page 26

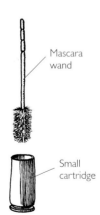

Mascara
wand

Small
cartridge

83

SLOP BUCKET

METHOD

Cut the eye drop phial to give a bucket shape, leaving ears sticking up at either side. Pierce these ears to take the handle. Thread the wire through a filigree link or a length of straw for a grip. Bend the wire to a handle shape and insert it through the holes in the ears. Top with a button, shaft uppermost.

MATERIALS

Eye drop phial
Wire
Long filigree link *or* straw
Button *or* dolls' house plate

Straw

Button

Wire

Eye drop phial cut down

Eye drop phial

From Housemaids' Slop Hopper, page 32

84

Mop Bucket

MATERIALS

Eyebath
Card
Perforated disc
Wire
Long link
Bead caps

METHOD

Cover one half of the eyebath with card and add a perforated disc to act as a sieve. Neaten the front edge of this cover with a further, thin strip of card. Attach a wire handle, bent to shape, threading it through a long link, for a grip, and through bead caps on either side of the bucket. Spray paint silver.

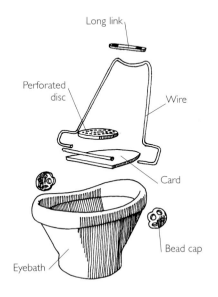

From Gentlemen's Municipal Urinal, page 62

85

Washbasins

SCENT BOTTLE TOP

METHOD

Cut the top off the chesspiece and glue the scent top in its place. Fix this pedestal on a decorative button or brooch finding. Cut a card surround and splashback for the basin. Spray paint the whole assembly silver. Fix a three-strand necklace fastener at the back for decoration, and add a tap made of solder, bent to shape, with a bead cap for a handle.

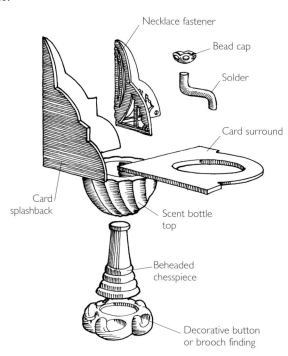

Necklace fastener

Bead cap

Solder

Card surround

Card splashback

Scent bottle top

Beheaded chesspiece

Decorative button or brooch finding

MATERIALS

Chesspiece
Scent bottle top
Card
Three-strand necklace
    fastener
Solder
Bead cap
Decorative button *or*
    brooch finding

From Ladies' Municipal Toilet, page 59

INDIVIDUAL PORTION JAM TUB

METHOD

Mount an individual portion jam tub on two pieces of balsa and add filigree bracelet links as brackets. Stick a press stud in place as a plughole. Make a splashback from another bracelet link or half a nurse's buckle. Spray both silver. Thread an earring stud through a long bead for the tap. Mount this on a washer and a second flat bead, and fix this to the centre of the nurse's buckle. Glue the sink in place, and add piping made from solder wire, bent to shape. Cut small strips of foil to hold the pipes in place on the wall. For the towel ring, pin a drop earring to the wall.

From Gentlemen's Municipal Urinal, page 62

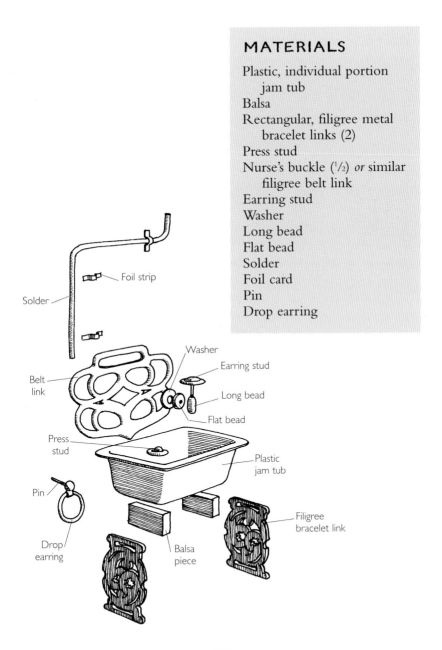

MATERIALS

Plastic, individual portion
    jam tub
Balsa
Rectangular, filigree metal
    bracelet links (2)
Press stud
Nurse's buckle ($^1/_2$) *or* similar
    filigree belt link
Earring stud
Washer
Long bead
Flat bead
Solder
Foil card
Pin
Drop earring

Solder

Foil strip

Washer

Earring stud

Belt
link

Long bead

Flat bead

Press
stud

Plastic
jam tub

Pin

Filigree
bracelet link

Drop
earring

Balsa
piece

SHELL

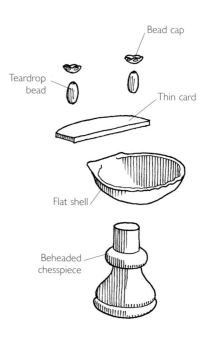

Bead cap

Teardrop bead

Thin card

Flat shell

Beheaded chesspiece

METHOD

Use the flat shell for a basin and mount it on a sawn-off chesspiece. Add a little shelf of card across the back to take the taps. Use teardrop beads for the taps with bead caps for the handles. (It helps to keep the taps straight if you thread them on a pin.) If you wish, add pierced earring caps for the spouts, as shown in the photo.

From Tinklebell Authentic Fairy's Toilet, page 74

MATERIALS

Flat shell
Wooden chesspiece
Thin card
Beadcaps
Teardrop-shaped beads
Pierced earring caps x 2

INDIVIDUAL PORTION BUTTER TUB

METHOD

Cut the butter tub in half and back one half with a shaped furniture decoration. For the tap, top a long bead with a bead cap, and thread them onto a pin. Cut two lengths of fan for the basin supports, and trim to shape. Glue the basin and the legs into place, and add an earring drop as a splashback.

MATERIALS

Individual portion butter tub
Shaped furniture decoration
Long bead
Bead cap
Pin
Plastic fan
Earring drop

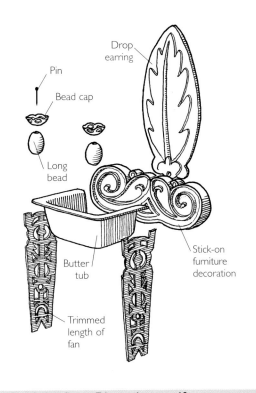

Drop earring
Pin
Bead cap
Long bead
Butter tub
Trimmed length of fan
Stick-on furniture decoration

From P. King Chinese Takeaway Loo, page 68

BUBBLE PACK
AN EXTRA, FLORAL WASHBASIN

METHOD

Cut the nib off the Stabilo Boss marker and use the casing for the pedestal. Use the bubble pack for the basin and decorate it and the pedestal with motifs cut from giftwrap. Add taps made from pierced earring caps, with beadcaps and tiny beads for handles, and attach the chain with a brass-headed tack. Attach two further earring caps inside the basin.

MATERIALS

Casing from Stabilo Boss
   highlighter
Small bubble pack,
   e.g. from screws
Giftwrap
Tiny chain
Pierced earring caps x 4
Beadcaps x 2
Tiny beads x 2
Brass-headed tack

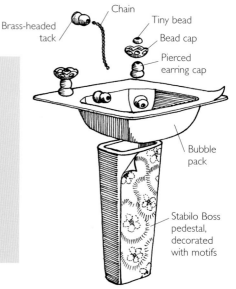

Chain
Brass-headed tack
Tiny bead
Bead cap
Pierced earring cap
Bubble pack
Stabilo Boss pedestal, decorated with motifs

MAKE-UP PACKAGING
AN EXTRA WASHBASIN, FULL OF WATER

MATERIALS

L'Oréal sublime make-up
  base packaging
Individual portion
  jam tub, oval
Cake pillar
Card
Necklace fastening
Chain
Pierced earring caps x 2
Bead caps x 2
Press studs x 2

METHOD

The middle tray from L'Oréal sublime make-up base compact makes an excellent washbasin top. Mount it on an individual portion jam tub, and then on a cake pillar cut to size. Cut a splashback from card, and decorate it with a necklace fastening. Add a chain, and make taps from pierced earring caps, with press studs for handles.

About the Author

An art teacher by profession, Patricia King has also worked as a display artist and window dresser, in an advertising art studio, and as a teacher of crafts and pottery. She is trained in stage design and continues to be involved with local amateur dramatic productions. She also arranges displays for art, craft and dolls' house exhibitions, and contributes a regular column to *Dolls' House World*.

This is Patricia's third book on dolls' house modelling. Her two previous titles, also published by GMC, are *Making Dolls' House Furniture* and *Making Victorian Dolls' House Furniture*. She lives in Surrey and is married with three children and a collection of grandchildren.

TITLES AVAILABLE FROM GMC PUBLICATIONS

BOOKS

WOODTURNING

Adventures in Woodturning	*David Springett*
Bert Marsh: Woodturner	*Bert Marsh*
Bill Jones' Notes from the Turning Shop	*Bill Jones*
Bill Jones' Further Notes from the Turning Shop	*Bill Jones*
Carving on Turning	*Chris Pye*
Colouring Techniques for Woodturners	*Jan Sanders*
Decorative Techniques for Woodturners	*Hilary Bowen*
Faceplate Turning: Features, Projects, Practice	*GMC Publications*
Green Woodwork	*Mike Abbott*
Illustrated Woodturning Techniques	*John Hunnex*
Keith Rowley's Woodturning Projects	*Keith Rowley*
Make Money from Woodturning	*Ann & Bob Phillips*
Multi-Centre Woodturning	*Ray Hopper*
Pleasure & Profit from Woodturning	*Reg Sherwin*
Practical Tips for Turners & Carvers	*GMC Publications*
Practical Tips for Woodturners	*GMC Publications*
Spindle Turning	*GMC Publications*
Turning Miniatures in Wood	*John Sainsbury*
Turning Wooden Toys	*Terry Lawrence*
Understanding Woodturning	*Ann & Bob Phillips*
Useful Woodturning Projects	*GMC Publications*
Woodturning: A Foundation Course	*Keith Rowley*
Woodturning Jewellery	*Hilary Bowen*
Woodturning Masterclass	*Tony Boase*
Woodturning: A Source Book of Shapes	*John Hunnex*
Woodturning Techniques	*GMC Publications*
Woodturning Wizardry	*David Springett*

WOODCARVING

The Art of the Woodcarver	*GMC Publications*
Carving Birds & Beasts	*GMC Publications*
Carving Realistic Birds	*David Tippey*
Carving on Turning	*Chris Pye*
Decorative Woodcarving	*Jeremy Williams*
Essential Woodcarving Techniques	*Dick Onians*
Lettercarving in Wood	*Chris Pye*
Practical Tips for Turners & Carvers	*GMC Publications*
Understanding Woodcarving	*GMC Publications*
Wildfowl Carving Volume 1	*Jim Pearce*
Wildfowl Carving Volume 2	*Jim Pearce*
The Woodcarvers	*GMC Publications*
Woodcarving: A Complete Course	*Ron Butterfield*
Woodcarving for Beginners: Projects, Techniques & Tools	*GMC Publications*
Woodcarving Tools, Materials & Equipment	*Chris Pye*

PLANS, PROJECTS, TOOLS & THE WORKSHOP

The Incredible Router	*Jeremy Broun*
Making & Modifying Woodworking Tools	*Jim Kingshott*
Sharpening: The Complete Guide	*Jim Kingshott*
Sharpening Pocket Reference Book	*Jim Kingshott*
The Workshop	*Jim Kingshott*

TOYS & MINIATURES

Designing & Making Wooden Toys	*Terry Kelly*
Fun to Make Wooden Toys & Games	*Jeff & Jennie Loader*
Making Wooden Toys & Games	*Jeff & Jennie Loader*
Making Board, Peg & Dice Games	*Jeff & Jennie Loader*
Making Little Boxes from Wood	*John Bennett*
Miniature Needlepoint Carpets	*Janet Granger*
Turning Miniatures in Wood	*John Sainsbury*
Turning Wooden Toys	*Terry Lawrence*

CREATIVE CRAFTS

Celtic Knotwork Designs	*Sheila Sturrock*
Collage from Seeds, Leaves and Flowers	*Joan Carver*
The Complete Pyrography	*Stephen Poole*
Creating Knitwear Designs	*Pat Ashforth & Steve Plummer*
Cross Stitch on Colour	*Sheena Rogers*
Embroidery Tips & Hints	*Harold Hayes*

CREATIVE CRAFTS *cont.*	Making Knitwear Fit	*Pat Ashforth & Steve Plummer*
	Miniature Needlepoint Carpets	*Janet Granger*
	Tatting Collage	*Lindsay Rogers*
UPHOLSTERY & FURNITURE	Care & Repair	*GMC Publications*
	Complete Woodfinishing	*Ian Hosker*
	Woodfinishing Handbook (Practical Crafts)	*Ian Hosker*
	Furniture Projects	*Rod Wales*
	Furniture Restoration (Practical Crafts)	*Kevin Jan Bonner*
	Furniture Restoration & Repair for Beginners	*Kevin Jan Bonner*
	Green Woodwork	*Mike Abbott*
	Making Fine Furniture	*Tom Darby*
	Making Shaker Furniture	*Barry Jackson*
	Pine Furniture Projects	*Dave Mackenzie*
	Seat Weaving (Practical Crafts)	*Ricky Holdstock*
	Upholsterer's Pocket Reference Book	*David James*
	Upholstery: A Complete Course	*David James*
	Upholstery: Techniques & Projects	*David James*
DOLLS' HOUSES & DOLLS' HOUSE FURNITURE	Architecture for Dolls' Houses	*Joyce Percival*
	A Beginners' Guide to the Dolls' House Hobby	*Jean Nisbett*
	The Complete Dolls' House Book	*Jean Nisbett*
	Easy-to-Make Dolls' House Accessories	*Andrea Barham*
	Make Your Own Dolls' House Furniture	*Maurice Harper*
	Making Dolls' House Furniture	*Patricia King*
	Making Period Dolls' House Accessories	*Andrea Barham*
	Making Period Dolls' House Furniture	*Derek & Sheila Rowbottom*
	Making Victorian Dolls' House Furniture	*Patricia King*
	Miniature Needlepoint Carpets	*Janet Granger*
	The Secrets of the Dolls' House Makers	*Jean Nisbett*
OTHER BOOKS	Guide to Marketing	*GMC Publications*
	Woodworkers' Career & Educational Source Book	*GMC Publications*

VIDEOS

Carving a Figure: The Female Form	*Ray Gonzalez*
The Traditional Upholstery Workshop Part 1: *Drop-in & Pinstuffed Seats*	*David James*
The Traditional Upholstery Workshop Part 2: *Stuffover Upholstery*	*David James*
Hollow Turning	*John Jordan*
Bowl Turning	*John Jordan*
Sharpening Turning & Carving Tools	*Jim Kingshott*
Sharpening the Professional Way	*Jim Kingshott*
Woodturning: A Foundation Course	*Keith Rowley*
Elliptical Turning	*David Springett*
Woodturning Wizardry	*David Springett*
Turning Between Centres: The Basics	*Dennis White*
Turning Bowls	*Dennis White*
Boxes, Goblets & Screw Threads	*Dennis White*
Novelties & Projects	*Dennis White*
Classic Profiles	*Dennis White*
Twists & Advanced Turning	*Dennis White*

MAGAZINES

WOODCARVING	BUSINESSMATTERS
WOODTURNING	FURNITURE & CABINETMAKING
TOYMAKING	CREATIVE IDEAS FOR THE HOME

The above represents a full list of all titles currently published or scheduled to be published. All are available direct from the Publishers or through bookshops, newsagents and specialist retailers. To place an order, or to obtain a complete catalogue, contact:

GMC Publications, 166 High Street, Lewes, East Sussex BN7 1XU United Kingdom
Tel: 01273 488005 Fax: 01273 478606

Orders by credit card are accepted